ALDRIDGE
IN OLD PHOTOGRAPHS

THESE VIEWS OF ALDRIDGE in the 1860s are the earliest known. The top photograph shows the Elms Hotel which was on one side of the High Street and the bottom photograph shows the Swan Inn which was on the opposite side of the road.

ALDRIDGE

IN OLD PHOTOGRAPHS

FROM THE JOHN SALE COLLECTION

COMPILED BY

JAN FARROW

FROM THE MEMORIES OF
STAN BROOKHOUSE AND OTHERS

ALAN SUTTON

Alan Sutton Publishing Limited
Phoenix Mill · Far Thrupp · Stroud · Gloucestershire

First published 1991

British Library Cataloguing in Publication Data

Aldridge in old photographs.
I. Sale, John II. Brookhouse, Stan
III. Farrow, Jan, *1943–*
942.49

ISBN 0-86299-972-3

Typeset in 9/10 Korinna.
Typesetting and origination by
Alan Sutton Publishing Limited.
Printed in Great Britain by
The Bath Press, Avon.

CONTENTS

INTRODUCTION

Through its history Aldridge has been spelt in many different ways. In the Domesday Book, where it is valued at 15s., it was called *Alrewic*. In medieval times there were many alder trees in the area and it is thought Aldridge may have got its name from these.

At the centre of the town is St Mary's Church, which was founded in the latter part of the twelfth century. The church has been altered several times over the centuries and the existing building is mainly in the Perpendicular style, with a Decorated tower. It was enlarged in 1853. The church contains two unusual thirteenth-century memorials. One is for Nicholas de Alrewiche, the reputed founder of the church; the other is for Sir Robert Stapleton who was Lord of the Manor. Sir Robert is represented in chain armour with a helmet and sword and it is probable that he fought in the Crusade of 1269. Memorial tablets for many other notable local individuals and families can be found in the church. Situated near the door is the parish bread box from which wheaten loaves were distributed to the poor who had attended both the service and the sermon. The church records date from 1660. At one time people were buried beneath the church and during excavations in 1991, when new flooring was put in, several coffins were found. One name-plate showed that they belonged to members of the Tongue family.

Aldridge's early prosperity depended on coal and beds of Etruria marl clay; the latter was particularly suited to the manufacture of blue bricks. Several collieries were opened in Aldridge in the 1860s and in 1878 Leighswood Colliery was producing good coal at 13s. 4d. a ton. Mining continued to be a major employer until the mid-1930s when the mines closed. Aldridge has been a producer of bricks for over 200 years. In the early part of this century there were several brickworks in Aldridge: Barnett & Beddows at the Atlas Works, John Beddows & Son at the Victoria Works, Aldridge Brick, Tile & Coal Company at the Utopia Works and the Joberns family at the Vigo Works. Bricks are still produced in Aldridge today, in two large modern factories.

In the early part of the century farming was also an important industry in the community – many people in Aldridge owned or worked on farms. Today Aldridge is the centre of much light industry and the large industrial estates house factories and industrial units.

There have always been a large number of schools in the area. Aldridge Free Grammar School was built in 1718. Revd Thomas Cooper gave land in trust so that a school might be built where children could be taught Anglican catechism, English and Latin tongues, and the writing of English. The Revd John Jordan, then Lord of the Manor of Aldridge, also endowed the school with land. The income from this land in 1822 was £115 10s. 0d. In 1759 the school was advertised as teaching mathematical sciences, particularly navigation or the art of sailing upon the sea. In 1829 it was decided that all sons of Aldridge should have free schooling between the ages of six and fourteen, but they still had to pay for pens, ink and copybooks.

In 1827 Cooper & Jordan Charity School was criticized by Charles Juxon, a militant reformer and overseer of the poor in Aldridge. He claimed that the schoolmaster Thomas Cook taught the children little or nothing and was so severe that few parents would send their children to the school. In 1833 Juxon declared, 'I defy the trustees or master to produce one person who has received an education which will fit him for the situation of schoolmaster or even manufacturer's clerk.' At one time the master of the school could take in boarders, and girls were taught by the master's wife. A charity fund was established that provided £12 a year for the education of girls, and in 1830 a meeting was held to nominate six poor girls between six and ten years of age to take advantage of the free places.

Cedar Court was built in 1792 and used as a boarding school for young ladies. At one time it had 50 boarders and was run by Mr and Mrs Allport. William Allport was listed in the Staffordshire General & Commercial Directory of 1818 as a 'School Master'. The fees were £26 a year for ordinary boarders and 50 guineas for parlour boarders. The pupils had to provide two sheets, six towels and a silver tablespoon and teaspoon. The syllabus included grammar and needlework and there were extra subjects which could be paid for each quarter. Fees for these subjects were as follows: Geography (with globes) 10s., French 21s., Drawing 21s. Pens were 10s. 6d. a quarter, and the pupils had to pay for laundry.

Revd James Lomax opened a school in 1804 at Druids Heath; its prospectus, which discussed health and diet at length, stated that 'as a drink at mealtimes good fresh beer would be allowed to any who choose it but water is far preferable for healthy children'. To prevent chilblains 'none but woollen stockings can be used by pupils from the first of October to the end of April; this rule however being subject to such modifications as the season may suggest'. The young gentlemen were not allowed to make secret visits to public houses, cottages, or other places in the neighbourhood 'where they may be drawn into expenses and form improper connections'. The rules forbade gambling and 'sport with gunpowder, firearms or offensive weapons'. The pupils were also ordered not to 'drink wine, spirits or fermented liquors without the knowledge of the conductor of the school'. Lomax aimed to fit pupils for commerce, the professions or university. Subjects included 'Euclid's elements of geometry, stenography, penmanship, navigation, parabolics or gunnery and astronomy', as well as basic subjects.

Aldridge still has a large number of schools. Cooper & Jordan Endowed Church of England School still exists, although now in a modern building. Aldridge County Secondary School was opened in 1953, and later moved to Tynings Lane, the same site as Aldridge Grammar School. The old Secondary School building became Leighswood Junior School, and now an infants' school has been built on the same campus. Redhouse and Whetstone Primary Schools serve the large new housing developments. St Mary of the Angels Primary School and St Francis of Assisi Comprehensive are the Catholic schools in the area. Aldridge Grammar and Secondary Schools have now merged to form Aldridge Comprehensive School.

Much of Aldridge has changed considerably, as the photographs in this book will show, but there are still good examples of old cottages and houses, not all of which can be included. In a walk round the Aldridge area one can discover a variety of interesting houses. Moot House, next to the church, is mid- to late-eighteenth-century and the cottage on the Croft dates from the same period. There are fine Victorian and Edwardian houses in Portland Road and Leighswood Road. Walsall Wood Road has a number of notable buildings, including Lea House, Noddy and Rose Cottages and Shutt Cross House; all these are still family dwellings. The first three of these are listed as buildings of historical interest in the Aldridge Conservation Area. Noddy and Rose Cottages may have been joined as a hatch connecting them was found during recent renovations. Two of the windows on the front of the cottages have been bricked up, presumably to avoid the payment of window tax. (This tax was introduced in 1697 and remained in force until 1851. It obliged the owners of buildings with ten windows to pay a tax on any additional windows.) At one time Rose Cottage had two wells, an ash-pit and a toilet with two seats (side-by-side) in the garden. Shutt Cross House is an imposing eighteenth-century building which had earlier origins as a farm house. It is a Grade II listed building, and in the large chimney at the back of the house there are footholds which were once used by chimney sweeps. Some of the windows in the house have also been bricked up. In the cellar there is a natural spring where the household obtained its water supply, and at one time there was a pond outside. The house was the home of Joseph Shutt who was curate of Aldridge church in 1825. Cedar Court, also in Walsall Wood Road, was bought by Frederick Tibbits in 1916. In those days the house was lit by oil lamps and candles and there were fires in all the rooms. The family employed twelve servants. The house has now been converted into several modern dwellings.

Aldridge in Old Photographs represents over fifteen years of collecting by John Sale, Stan Brookhouse and myself. The idea of the book came into being when we decided that it was important to share our collections with Aldridge residents. Realizing that many old photographs end up in dustbins or lie hidden and forgotten in the bottom of drawers, we felt fortunate to have a pictorial history at our fingertips. By putting these photographs together in a book we hoped to make them available for all of Aldridge's population to enjoy. John Sale and Stan Brookhouse have spent many years taking and collecting photographs of people and places which would otherwise have disappeared without trace. They have also organized slide shows on Aldridge's recent past which have given pleasure to a great many people. We hope *Aldridge in Old Photographs* will be just as successful.

Much of the information in this book is based on the memories of old Aldridge residents. Whilst every effort has been made to ensure the accuracy of the facts given, we are aware that there will be occasions when readers will disagree with someone else's personal recollection. We apologize for any such errors and hope that they will in no way detract from enjoyment of the book.

SECTION ONE
The Village Centre

THIS VIEW OF THE HIGH STREET, c. 1908, shows the fountain with the water trough. Horses used the trough and, according to one old resident, circus animals were also watered there when passing through the village.

THIS VIEW OF THE FOUNTAIN, c. 1920, shows the change from gas to electric lighting and the addition of several more direction boards to the signpost. The house behind the trees was called the Chestnuts and it housed Belgian refugees during the First World War.

CHURCH PARADE, C. 1905, taken looking down Anchor Road. The fair can be seen behind the bushes on the right; it came to Aldridge each September for 'Wakes Week'.

A SIGNPOST replaces the old fountain and horse trough, seen here in 1954.

MAKING THE NEW ROAD AT NORTHGATE. A Harper's bus can be seen coming from Walsall Wood Road and negotiating the island on which Mr Marriot's house stands. Mr Marriot's house was used as a temporary post office while the new post office was being built in Northgate.

A VIEW LOOKING UP THE HIGH STREET taken in 1969, with some recent new developments on the right-hand side.

THIS VIEW OF THE ISLAND was taken from a crane during the construction of Homebell House in 1987.

THE ANCHOR INN which stood at the corner of Walsall Wood Road and High Street.

ALDRIDGE HIGH STREET during the 1950s or '60s.

THE HIGH STREET in c. 1904. On the left is Aston's bread shop with the bread cart outside.

THE OLD SWAN INN in Aldridge High Street.

THOMAS POTTS' STORE. Mr Potts lived at Shutt Cross House. Mr Hilditch, who worked for Mr Potts when he was a young man, later took over the business.

Thomas Potts,

Grocer & Ironmonger,

WINE & SPIRIT MERCHANT.

Agent for FLOWERS', ALLSOP'S, WHITBREAD'S, TRUMAN
AND HANBURY'S

ALES, STOUT, AND LAGER BEER,

In Cask and Bottle.

Ransome & Simms' Lawn Mowers

STAR CYCLES.

AN ADVERTISEMENT FOR THOMAS POTTS' STORE which appeared in a parish magazine of 1908.

ANOTHER VIEW OF THOMAS POTTS' STORE. The advertisements painted on the end of the building are for Priory Tea, Flower and Sons' Stratford Ales, and Truman, Hanbury and Buxton's Burton Ales and Stout. The shop was established in 1868.

JOSEPH HILDITCH took over Thomas Potts' store in 1923. Notice the display case of Sheffield steel knives on the wall outside the shop.

A LATER VIEW OF HILDITCH & SON still advertises Truman, Hanbury & Buxton's Burton Ale.

HILDITCH'S SHOP WINDOW decorated for the jubilee of George V in 1935.

HILDITCH'S SHOP in 1937, with Joseph Hilditch left, Eric Pritchard and George Burnett. The shop closed in 1983 when his grandson Reg Hilditch retired.

THE OLD ELMS. This building was demolished in 1954 for High Street redevelopment. It was used as a food office in the Second World War and is reported to have been over 200 years old. Old residents recall it being open for long hours to accommodate waggons and brakes that passed through the village. In those days the licensee had to fetch water from the village pump at the corner of Walsall Wood Road.

ANOTHER VIEW OF THE ELMS HOTEL, which was situated opposite Bakers Lane. The inn brewed its own beer.

ALDRIDGE HIGH STREET in the early 1900s. There was a slaughter house opposite the Elms, next to the butchers.

TED BUCKLEY'S BAKERS SHOP. The shop stood at the corner of Bakers Lane and High Street. It is said that at Christmas some Aldridge residents took their turkeys to Ted Buckley so that he could cook them in his large ovens. They were then collected as people returned from morning service on Christmas Day.

ALDRIDGE HIGH STREET IN c. 1950.

ALDRIDGE POST OFFICE IN C. 1910.

CRUCK COTTAGES IN THE HIGH STREET. The first Aldridge telephone exchange was in these cottages.

DEMOLITION OF THE CRUCK COTTAGES in the 1960s. These medieval houses were the only known cruck-trussed houses in the Aldridge area.

ALDRIDGE HIGH STREET. The cottages in the foreground were used by the British Legion.

ALDRIDGE HIGH STREET in about 1904, showing Aston's bread shop and the cruck cottages.

THE MANOR COTTAGES, c.1911. They were part of the Manor House estate and were sold in 1928 to the British Legion.

ALDRIDGE HIGH STREET. Alice Potts, a nurse at the Manor House auxiliary hospital, is said to have lived in one of these white cottages.

ALDRIDGE HIGH STREET in the early 1960s.

SECTION TWO

Industry

LEIGHSWOOD COLLIERY, known as the No. 2 plant and nicknamed 'Drybones'.

THE 'BASIN', BRICKYARD ROAD showing the remains of the bridge where coal was loaded onto barges.

LOADING THE COAL WAGGONS at Leighswood Colliery No. 2 plant. The first pit at Aldridge was the 'Victoria' trial pit. It was sunk in 1849 in a field near Middlemore Lane, then Speedwell Lane. In later years it was used as an air-shaft for the two larger pits known as No. 1 pit, nicknamed 'Drybread', and No. 2, 'Drybones'. Both pits were sunk in the 1870s and were 1,400 feet deep. They both closed in the '30s.

ALDRIDGE NO. 1 PLANT was situated near Boatmans Lane and was owned by the Aldridge Brick, Tile & Coal Co. Ltd. The building in the foreground contained the fan which ventilated the pit.

THIS ADVERTISEMENT for Aldridge Brick, Tile & Coal Company appeared in the 1948 'All Star Variety Souvenir Programme'.

ALDRIDGE BRICK, TILE & COAL COMPANY WORKS. The chimney in the distance is that of the Joberns' brickworks.

ALDRIDGE COAL MERCHANT, Mr Cooper (right) with his waggoners. The man in the centre is Jackie Brown. This photograph was taken in Aldridge sidings behind the station. Coal was brought from Aldridge and Walsall Wood Collieries then unloaded into horse-drawn carts.

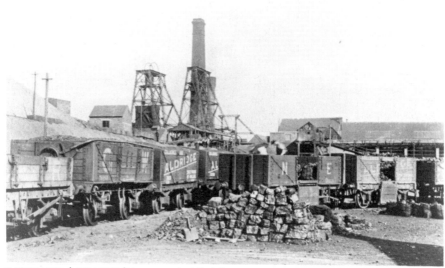

ALDRIDGE NO. 1 COLLIERY. It is suggested that the wages were so poor that the men only took dry bread to work for their lunch, hence the nickname 'Drybread'.

A LETTER-HEAD from the Aldridge Colliery Co. Ltd.

ALDRIDGE MINE RESCUE TEAM.

STEAM-POWERED COAL WAGGONS owned by Aldridge Colliery Company. They were used just after the Second World War to deliver 'allowance coal' to the miners' houses.

ALDRIDGE NO. 1 'DRYBREAD' COLLIERY. Many Aldridge men and boys worked 'down the pit'.

THE SOUP KITCHEN photographed at the Red Lion, Aldridge during the 1926 pit strike. Children would go there from school to get their lunch.

THE COPPY HALL COLLIERY at Stubbers Green which for some years was run by Edward Barnett.

THE LAST PAY DAY at Aldridge Colliery, 1936.

A DRAGLINE DIGGER AT WORK at Aldridge Brick, Tile & Coal Co. Ltd, 1952. Clay quarried here by mechanical digger was earlier dug by hand.

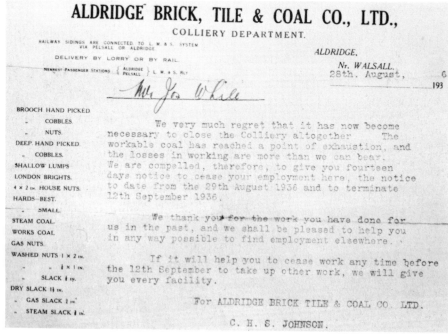

ALDRIDGE BRICK, TILE & COAL CO., LTD.,
COLLIERY DEPARTMENT.

RAILWAY SIDINGS ARE CONNECTED TO L. M. & S. SYSTEM
VIA PELSALL OR ALDRIDGE.

DELIVERY BY LORRY OR BY RAIL.

NEAREST PASSENGER STATIONS { ALDRIDGE / PELSALL } L. M. & S. RLY

ALDRIDGE,
Nr. WALSALL,
28th. August,   6.
_____193

Mr Jos While

BROOCH HAND PICKED
- COBBLES.
- NUTS.
DEEP. HAND PICKED.
- COBBLES.
SHALLOW LUMPS
LONDON BRIGHTS.
4 × 2 IN. HOUSE NUTS.
HARDS—BEST.
- SMALL.
STEAM COAL.
WORKS COAL.
GAS NUTS.
WASHED NUTS 1 × 2 IN.
- " ½ × 1 IN.
- SLACK ½ IN.
DRY SLACK 1½ IN.
- GAS SLACK ½ IN.
- STEAM SLACK ½ IN.

We very much regret that it has now become necessary to close the Colliery altogether The workable coal has reached a point of exhaustion, and the losses in working are more than we can bear. We are compelled, therefore, to give you fourteen days notice to cease your employment here, the notice to date from the 29th August 1936 and to terminate 12th September 1936.

We thank you for the work you have done for us in the past, and we shall be pleased to help you in any way possible to find employment elsewhere.

If it will help you to cease work any time before the 12th September to take up other work, we will give you every facility.

For ALDRIDGE BRICK TILE & COAL CO. LTD.

C. H. S. JOHNSON.

A LETTER FROM ALDRIDGE BRICK, TILE & COAL CO. LTD dated 28 August 1936 which gave notice to Mr While. When the supplies of coal ceased to make the colliery viable it closed.

A CLAYHOLE at the Atlas Brickworks of Barnett & Beddows, with the Empire Brickworks in the background, c. 1940.

WORKERS REMOVING THE 'OVERBURDEN' at Aldridge brickyard. The overburden was the layer of soil which was removed before exposing the clay.

A VIEW OF KILNS AT the brickworks, Aldridge.

BARNETT & BEDDOWS' ATLAS BRICKWORKS. The workers are packing a consignment of bricks for Tasmania.

JOHN BROOKES, BRICKYARD WORKER, taking bricks to the kiln.

BARNETT & BEDDOWS, Ltd.

Atlas Brick Works,

Stubber's Green, ALDRIDGE, Nr. Walsall

MAKERS OF :—

BLUE
STAFFORDSHIRE BRICKS

PRESSED AND WIRECUT

ALSO

BRINDLED AND HARD RED WIRECUTS

Phone : 52218 ALDRIDGE

AN ADVERTISEMENT FOR BARNETT & BEDDOWS which appeared in 'The All Star Variety Souvenir Programme' for Wednesday 27 October 1948. Local people took part in these shows and the proceeds went to charity. The proceeds from this show went to the Over Sixty Club.

TAKING BRICKS FROM THE PRESSES to the kilns. Small mechanical trucks carry the bricks on stillages and leave them in the kiln for setting. Wheelbarrows were used for this job.

A SANDBLAST MACHINE at Aldridge Brick, Tile & Coal Co. Ltd brickworks. This machine gave a rough texture and pleasant colour to bricks to be used for facing work. It gave bricks a 'hand made' appearance at less cost.

FLEET OF LORRIES at Aldridge Brickworks, c. 1950.

THE VIGO BRICKWORKS near Walsall Wood was owned by the Joberns family. The clay dug here was said to be of inferior quality to that of the other brickworks.

THE DEMOLITION OF THE CHIMNEY at Aldridge Brick, Tile & Coal Company in the early 1940s when it was believed that German bombers were using it as a 'fix' or navigation aid. Today there are two brickworks in Aldridge: Ibstock Brick, who took over Aldridge Brick, Tile & Coal Company in 1965, and the new brickworks of Christian Salvesen which is on the land once owned by Barnett & Beddows.

HENRY REECE,

Wharf Cottage,

Aldridge,

Having a Horse and Cart, would be pleased to receive Orders for Drawing Coal, and General Hauling.

ADVERTISEMENT FOR HENRY REECE, 'Haulage Contractor', 1908.

Farms and Farming

MANOR FARM, ALDRIDGE was situated close to the Manor House.

OUTSIDE MANOR FARM, c. 1897. From left to right: Samuel Robinson Bonner, Mary Elizabet, Jackie Middleton, Helen Dorothy Bonner and Ursula Catherine Bonner.

ALDRIDGE CATTLE MARKET was held at the rear of this building at the beginning of this century. The building was also used as an 'outdoor'.

WHITE HOUSE FARM once stood on the site now occupied by the White House public house.

THE FARM IN ROOKERY LANE. The house was situated where the entrance ramp to Safeways car park is today. It was farmed by Mr Bannister, 'Lord Rookery', between 1914 and 1930.

TED BANNISTER and his dog outside Rookery Farm in about 1920.

COPPY HALL FARM.

GRANGE FARM, Walton Road was last occupied by the Ferries family.

THE VILLAGE BLACKSMITHS, Fuller Thomas and Harry Pointon. The forge was situated at the junction of Walsall Road and Birmingham Road.

CHILDREN RIDING with Mr Judson on Fred Tibbits' hay-cart. This photograph was taken in the 1930s in the fields at the rear of the old council houses in Walsall Wood Road.

BASSFORD'S COTTAGES stood at the corner of Whetstone Lane and Portland Road. They were demolished in 1962.

THE BASSFORD BROTHERS, George, Jack and Charlie at the rear of the Bassford cottages.

BARNS AT NODDY PARK FARM which have recently been converted into houses.

MANOR FARM COTTAGE in the winter of 1947.

WALTER HERBERT, waggoner, in Noddy Park, c. 1930. Cedar Court can be seen in the background.

GEORGE HERBERT ploughing with a horse-drawn plough.

FARM LABOURER Albert Boulton picking potatoes in the Longwood Road area.

A THRESHING MACHINE at harvest-time on an Aldridge farm.

Transport

THE 2.15 TO BIRMINGHAM at Aldridge station in 1955.

ALDRIDGE STATION with the station staff looking toward Anchor Bridge.

ALDRIDGE STATION was opened in July 1879 and this view was taken in the early 1900s. The small train in the centre is the branch-line train that ran from Brownhills via Walsall Wood. The other train on the main line to Walsall was returning from Birmingham. The branch line between Aldridge, Walsall Wood and Brownhills, a distance of four miles, began operating in 1884. In 1899 this service was operating three passenger trains a day and five on Saturdays. The branch line was a single track with various 'spur' lines off to collieries and brickworks in the area. It is interesting to note that during the Second World War the train carrying King George VI and Queen Elizabeth to Birmingham after the Blitz stopped in the sidings at Aldridge.

AN EARLY VIEW OF ALDRIDGE STATION. In 1930 it cost 1½d. return to Walsall and 10d. return to Birmingham New Street. There were services to Sutton Park and many children went on their Sunday School treat by train to the Park.

ALDRIDGE STATION STAFF taken during the 1914–18 war when women were employed as staff for the first time. The station-master was Mr Gilbert, seated in the middle of the row. The station-master lived in a large house in Leighswood Road (see p. 60).

A GOODS TRAIN with coal trucks on the branch line.

A GOODS TRAIN derailed on 30 August 1960 on the branch line which ran from Aldridge via Walsall Wood.

ALDRIDGE SIGNAL BOX.

INSIDE ALDRIDGE SIGNAL BOX.

THE VIEW FROM THE SIGNAL BOX towards Station Bridge.

THE LAST PASSENGER TRAIN which ran from Aldridge to Birmingham on 16 January 1965. The closure was a result of the Beeching 'axe'.

THE STATION WAS BOARDED UP in the late 1960s and later demolished.

THE STATION-MASTER'S HOUSE. This house was situated in Leighswood Road and has recently been demolished.

THE ASTON, PARKES AND HILDITCH FAMILIES in one of Aldridge's first motor cars. The Star Motor Company started building cars in 1898 and their first car cost 180 guineas.

A GROUP OF CYCLISTS in c. 1910, all members of the Bassford family.

AN EARLY MOTORBIKE at Hobs Hole Lane, 1906.

A BRAKE OUTSIDE ALDRIDGE CHURCH. Trips were common in the summer months; the horse-drawn hearse at the rear carried the food and drink. There seem to be at least nineteen people on board the coach.

THE CANAL LOCKS and lock-keeper's cottage seen from the bridge at the junction of Longwood Lane and Walsall Road.

A STEAM LORRY taking ammunition from Streetly works to Aldridge station during the First World War. Mr Phillips is the driver.

MR CLAPTON with a steamroller belonging to Aldridge Urban District Council. Mr Clapton won a medal for action behind enemy lines during the 1914–18 war.

BILLY BUNN outside his garage in Paddock Lane which opened in 1921. At that time he was one of three car owners in the village. During the war the building on the left was used as an auxiliary fire station.

THE GARAGE later moved to Walsall Road. This photograph taken in 1939 shows the multi-pump which served five types of petrol. Harold Moore, garage mechanic, is serving the petrol.

ALBERT LOTE AND ARTHUR WOOD in their three-wheeled Morgan which they bought second-hand for £5 in 1929. The photograph was taken at the rear of Northwood Villas in Leighswood Road.

SAMMY JONES' LORRY. He started a haulage company on Walsall Wood Road with a horse and cart and the company grew. It is now Jones Transport.

FRANK JAMES' HILL GARAGE in Little Aston Road.

FRANK JAMES' HILL GARAGE or the Garage, seen here before its recent conversion into houses. The building is now known as the Maltings.

ALDRIDGE'S FIRST AMBULANCE, a Morris, outside the Manor House in 1949.

LEIGHSWOOD ROW with one of the first cars to be owned by people in these houses. These houses were originally built for miners who worked at the local pits.

THE HARPER BROTHERS operated the first bus service from Aldridge to Cannock. They had a fleet of single- and double-deck buses with a livery of green and cream. The photograph shows Harper's Goria Deluxe Bus at the island in Aldridge.

HARPER BROTHERS' GARAGE in Anchor Road. The building was later taken over by Simulox Tyres and is now vacant.

ALDRIDGE AIRPORT during the Second World War. Spitfires and Harvards came to the airport for repairs at 'Helliwell's Factory'.

THE LAST AEROPLANE repaired at Helliwell's seen here with the Helliwell's staff and Roger Mills the test pilot.

Celebrations

ALDRIDGE HIGH STREET with the church in the background and Hudson's drapers on the right, during the celebrations for the coronation of George V in 1911.

MAYPOLE DANCING at Cedar Court.

THE END OF THE PIT STRIKE in 1926. This photograph was taken outside the Co-op in Station Road and the children are dressed in food bags.

PORTLAND ROAD decorated for the coronation of George V in 1911.

ALDRIDGE CONSERVATIVE CLUB at the end of Rookery Lane where the library is today. This photograph was taken in 1911 and the building is decorated for the coronation celebrations.

THE CROFT as it was in 1911. Grouped round the bandstand from left to right are several prominent Aldridge men: Mr Marriot, Mr Myring, Mr H.G. Walker, Mr Stephens, Mr S. Bonner and Mr Myring.

ALDRIDGE HIGH STREET decorated for the coronation of George V.

A CARNIVAL PROCESSION waiting at Aldridge station in 1937.

MR JUDSON leading the 'Blossom Time' float as it passes Cedar Court.

ALDRIDGE CARNIVAL 1937. The ceremony of crowning the Carnival Queen was performed by Howard Walton (centre) who was a well-known Aldridge man. He was captain of Aldridge cricket team, a local farmer and a councillor. The Carnival Queen, Nancy Judson, had four attendants. From left to right: Miss Geogan, Miss Chadwick, Iris Brown and Lily Hough. This photograph was taken outside the Council House, Anchor Road.

THE CARNIVAL KING passes the Elms Hotel in a horse-drawn carriage. The proceeds from the Carnival in 1937 went to the Aldridge Nursing Association.

THE CORONATION OF GEORGE VI. This photograph of the procession was taken at the junction of Station Road and Paddock Lane in front of Davies' shop.

CELEBRATIONS for the silver jubilee of King George V. The procession is passing the Elms in the High Street.

CELEBRATIONS FOR THE CORONATION OF GEORGE V IN 1911. This group is outside Thomas Potts' shop and the children are holding their coronation mugs.

INTERIOR OF THE ASSEMBLY ROOMS.

CHILDREN ON A ROUNDABOUT on the Croft during the coronation celebrations in 1953. Rookery Lane is on the left.

THIS COUPLE are standing by the fountain which stood at the junction of Leighswood Road, Anchor Road and High Street. A plaque above them was inscribed as follows: 'This fountain was erected by the inhabitants of Aldridge to celebrate the Diamond Jubilee of the Reign of Queen Victoria 1897'. The fountain was removed in the 1950s.

THE WEDDING of Guy James, son of Frank James.

THE STONE-LAYING CEREMONY for the Methodist Church in Anchor Road, July 1934. Aldridge became an urban district council in this year and the new Council House can be seen in the background.

THE BAND at the stone-laying ceremony of Anchor Road Methodist Church.

ALDRIDGE COLLIERY SILVER PRIZE BAND.

THE DEDICATION OF THE BRITISH LEGION STANDARD at Cedar Court Meadow 1949. The Methodist minister was Revd E.J. Turner.

SECTION SIX

Religion

THE INTERIOR OF ALDRIDGE CHURCH showing the Jacobean-style pulpit, and the eagle lectern. The pews were removed in 1991. On the wall on each side of the altar are written the Ten Commandments and the Lord's Prayer.

ALDRIDGE SUNDAY SCHOOL CERTIFICATE.

ALDRIDGE CHURCH and the Manor Farm duck pond, c. 1934.

ALDRIDGE CHURCH, C. 1908. The man with the donkey-cart is selling blocks of salt.

BLESSING OF THE CENOTAPH by the Bishop of Lichfield with Revd Tarleton. The Cenotaph was in the churchyard before it was moved to its present site in the late 1950s.

THE PARISH CHURCH and Manor Farm in an early photograph.

WATCH AND CLOCKMAKER D.W. Heitzman was responsible for winding and repairing the Aldridge church clock.

DEMOLISHING the wall around the Croft prior to the construction of the new road in the 1950s.

THE CENOTAPH AND MANOR FARM. This area was originally part of the Croft.

ALMS HOUSES built with a donation from Mrs Walker and situated off Erdington Road close to Bay Tree House.

ALDRIDGE RECTORY was built in the 1820s. After remaining derelict for a long period it was converted and became part of an old people's home.

THE MOTHERS UNION with the Revd Tarleton and his wife on the front step of the Rectory.

SUNDAY TEA on the vicarage lawn in c. 1940. The Rectory had an additional wing at that time. These people were probably listening to music by the Aldridge Colliery Band.

SOME LOCAL WESLEYANS building a wall at the rear of the Wesleyan chapel. Standing, from left to right: Harry Cotton, Mr Millington, Mr Wright, Sammy Jones, the minister, Mr Marriot, -?-, -?-. Seated: Mr Crumpton, -?-, -?-, Harold Love, -?-.

THE WESLEYAN CHAPEL in Walsall Wood Road.

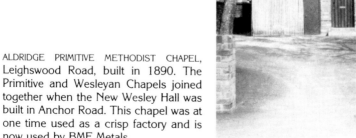

ALDRIDGE PRIMITIVE METHODIST CHAPEL, Leighswood Road, built in 1890. The Primitive and Wesleyan Chapels joined together when the New Wesley Hall was built in Anchor Road. This chapel was at one time used as a crisp factory and is now used by BMF Metals.

Bethesda
Primitive Methodist
Chapel
Leighs Wood.

Special

Prize

AWARDED TO
Cyril Jukes.

FOR

The Cleanest Card
during the year 1909.

B.Clare Supt:
E. Jukes. Sety:
March 22nd 1910

A BOOK-PLATE in a book awarded as a prize at the Primitive Methodist Chapel.

THE METHODIST CHAPEL in Anchor Road in 1940.

THE WESLEYAN CHAPEL ANNIVERSARY in 1948.

THE METHODIST CHAPEL IN ANCHOR ROAD.

Schools

THE SCHOOL COTTAGES were latterly used by the school caretaker but originally in 1718 this building housed Aldridge Grammar School.

LOOKING TOWARDS 'THE GREEN' SCHOOL. The original Grammar School was endowed by the Revds Thomas Cooper and John Jordan and became known as Cooper & Jordan Endowed School.

ALDRIDGE ENDOWED SCHOOL IN 1959.

THE PERCUSSION BAND with Miss Long at Cooper & Jordan School, c. 1930.

ALDRIDGE INFANTS' SCHOOL IN 1923.

ALDRIDGE INFANTS' SCHOOL IN 1937.

MISS BIRCHER AND MISS DAVIS with their class at Cooper & Jordan Infants' School in the 1930s.

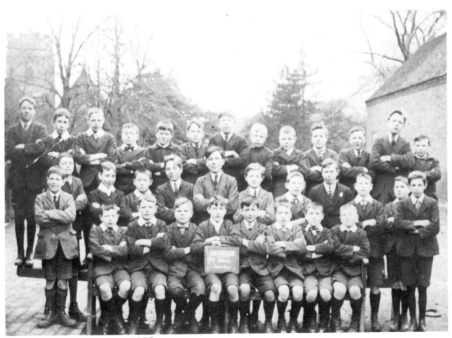

ALDRIDGE BOYS' SCHOOL IN 1922.

ALDRIDGE BOYS' SCHOOL at the turn of the century.

THIS ORPHANAGE was built by the Royal Antediluvian Order of Buffaloes and was opened in 1904 by Local Chief Justice, Lord Alverstone. In 1907 the honorary secretary Leonard Aulton sent an appeal, using postcards of the orphanage, to every brother and friend of the Order for contributions towards a target of £500 for the sanatorium building fund. Additional wings were also built in 1921.

A VIEW INSIDE THE ORPHANAGE dated October 1905.

THE ORPHANAGE was later taken over by Dr Barnardo's and the building was demolished in 1965. The modern single storey building of the Cedar School now occupies the site.

OPENING OF THE CEDAR SCHOOL in February 1986. Kate Upton presents a flower to the Princess of Wales while her mother and sister Emma look on. The Cedar School is now empty; the land and building have been sold for possible housing development.

COUNTY COUNCIL OF STAFFORDSHIRE
EDUCATION COMMITTEE

CANNOCK CHASE DIVISIONAL EXECUTIVE
ALDRIDGE COUNTY SECONDARY SCHOOL

OFFICIAL OPENING

by

Councillor J. A. Robson

Chairman of the Staffordshire County Education
Committee, on

Thursday 26th March, 1953

THE BENHILL PRESS LIMITED, RUGELEY, STAFFS.

ALDRIDGE COUNTY SECONDARY SCHOOL opened in 1953. Later in the 1950s it became Leighswood Junior School and the Secondary School moved to its present Tynings Lane site.

CEDAR COURT, once the home of the Allport family, was used as a school and in later years was the home of the Tibbits family. It has recently been converted into flats.

COPPY HALL was originally built as a school and Mr Lomax was a headteacher. The school later moved to Druids Heath. It was at one time the home of Mr Partridge, the Clerk of the Urban District Council.

ALDRIDGE CHURCH OF ENGLAND SCHOOL class 3, c. 1920. The teacher, Mrs Sambrook, is standing at the back of the class. Among the pupils are Floss Hathaway, Kathy Frost, Dolly Whitehouse, Violet Roberts, Violet Haden, Ethel Pointon, Enid Brookhouse, Florrie Judson and Ethel Thomas.

Sport and Leisure

ALDRIDGE HOCKEY TEAM, c. 1930. Back row, left to right: ? Brown, L. Pearson, -?-, Tom Tibbits, K. Leech, E. Sheldon, ? Bayliss. Middle row: M. Rayment, Bert Partridge, J. Francis, N. Evans, Bill Minors, -?-, N. Bush, C. Holland, J. Smith. Seated: Bob Cox, J. Russell, B. Franks, H. Walton, W. Holland, G. Bird, -?-, Manager of the Elms. Dicky Bonnett sits cross-legged on the ground. Fred Tibbits, wearing the bowler hat, is in the centre of the picture. Dicky Bonnett, co-founder of Buxton & Bonnett gents' outfitters in Walsall, made a bet that 200 spectators would be present to watch the match and then invited the orphanage boys in order to win his bet.

ALDRIDGE FOOTBALL TEAM in early days.

ALDRIDGE HOCKEY TEAM IN C. 1940. Back row, left to right: David Partridge, George Bird, Bob Robson, Bill Robson, ? Ballinger, Norman Bush. Front row: Arnold Ballinger, Ken Leach, Harry Baker, -?-, Les Pearson.

DR VICTOR MILNE who played centre-half for Aston Villa 1924–8. He played in the 1924 Cup Final when Villa lost to Newcastle, 2–0. He also played cricket for Aldridge and on one occasion in 1926 took 10 wickets for 17 runs.

ALDRIDGE OLD BOYS' FOOTBALL CLUB, 1925–6. Back row, left to right: Jack Plant, Bill Jones, Fred Robins, Joe Lynch, Len Brookes, Ernie Page, Jim Davis, Billy Bunn. Middle row: Malcolm Raymond, Jack Harvey, Fred Foster, Walter Hastilow, Charlie Holland. Front row: Charlie Page, Charlie Milner, Sam Brookes.

JOHNNY LEWIS who played football for West Bromwich Albion and later for Mansfield Town.

ALDRIDGE CRICKET CLUB, C. 1920. This picture was taken outside the Rectory.

HOWARD WALTON, Captain of Aldridge Cricket Club.

111

ALDRIDGE LADIES' HOCKEY TEAM IN c. 1910.

PLAYING BOWLS on the Old Elms bowling green. The buildings in the background are the shops in Aldridge High Street. The picture may have been taken on a Thursday afternoon, local shop-keepers' early closing day.

CHARLIE, JACK AND ALF HOLLAND on their 'Tridom'.

CHARLIE HOLLAND (1908–1989) represented England as a cyclist in the 1932 Los Angeles Olympic Games and in Berlin in 1936. He won a bronze medal in 1932 for the 4000m team pursuit.

JOHNNY BULLOCK, an Aldridge man, was rider of the Grand National winner 'Nickel Coin' in 1951.

CHARLIE WARD, also an Aldridge man, was a professional golfer at Sutton Coldfield and Little Aston Clubs. He was a member of the Ryder Cup team in the 1940s and won 60 major championships in his lifetime.

AVION SUPER CINEMA DE LUXE ALDRIDGE

Special Opening Programme

MONDAY, SEPTEMBER 26th, at 2-30 p.m.

(This Programme is retained for Tuesday and Wednesday, September 27th and 28th)

NATIONAL ANTHEM

OPENING CEREMONY
BY
HIS WORSHIP
THE MAYOR OF WALSALL
Supported by the Chairman and Members of the
Aldridge Urban District Council

GEORGE HOUSTON
in the Adventure story

· WALLABY JIM ·
OF THE ISLANDS
(U)

4.   BRITISH MOVIETONE NEWS

5.   Personal Appearance of that Great Film Star

Mr. GEORGE FORMBY
Who is presenting a Cheque to the Mayor of Walsall
for the Walsall Hospitals Fund

6.   Now See him in his Latest Picture

GEORGE FORMBY
in
I SEE ICE·
(U)

THE AVION CINEMA was opened on Monday 26 September 1938 by George Formby.

THE INTERIOR of the Avion Cinema. This view of the lounge was featured in the souvenir programme.

HARRY RUSSEL, Manager of the Avion Cinema, with one of Mr Loverock's donkeys. The donkey would often stray to the Avion where he was given chocolate by the staff at the ticket desk.

THE AVION CINEMA had double seats. They can be seen on the left of this picture.

THE ALDRIDGE SHOW. The last Aldridge Flower Show was held on Bank Holiday Monday at Cedar Court in 1966. In the centre of this picture is one of Mr Loverock's donkeys.

THE HUNT AT NUTTALL'S FARM.

THE SWAN OUTING to the Shrewsbury Flower Show in 1920. They travelled by charabanc.

THIS ADVERTISEMENT for Johnsons' Preserves appeared in the Walsall Red Book for 1937.

ALDRIDGE SCHOOL BOYS on an outing. The bus is one of Harper's fleet and the railway station can be seen in the background.

A DAY TRIP to the seaside by the Aldridge British Legion, 1952.

ALDRIDGE GIRL GUIDES in c. 1920 with their leader Mrs Brown. Mrs Brown lived at Lea House, Walsall Wood Road.

THE GIRL GUIDES assembled on the Croft to celebrate their golden jubilee in 1960.

The War Years

NURSES AND SOLDIERS DURING THE FIRST WORLD WAR in the gardens of the Manor House which was used as an auxiliary hospital. Nurse Potts is in the centre of the back row. A plaque to her memory is in Aldridge Church.

ALDRIDGE SPECIAL POLICE during the Second World War, outside Aldridge Police Station.

THE DAVIS FAMILY at the back of their cottage in Brickyard Row. The photograph was taken during the First World War.

LADIES OF THE HOME GUARD on parade on the Croft. Mrs Harding, who was in charge of the food office in the Old Elms during the Second World War, is among those on parade.

OFFICERS OF THE HOME GUARD during the Second World War. Back row, left to right: -?-, -?-, -?-, -?-, Harry Wadsworth, -?-, -?-, Mr Hazzard. Front row: -?-, Percy Stevens, Bill Howarth, Mr Davis.

A LARGE CRATER MADE BY THE FIRST BOMB to be dropped in the area during the Second World War, at Daw End, Rushall.

A ROYAL AIR FORCE BOMBER which overshot the runway at the airport on 14 July 1938.

WARSHIP WEEK 31st. Jan.—7th. Feb. 1942.

PLAQUE
presented to the
Urban District
of Aldridge by
the Lords Com-
missioners of
the Admiralty

PLAQUE
presented to
H.M. Motor
Torpedo Boat,
No. 71, by the
Citizens of the
Urban District
of Aldridge.

SOUVENIR

IN APPRECIATION OF THE SUCCESSFUL EFFORT OF SAVINGS WORKERS IN ALDRIDGE URBAN DIS-
TRICT IN RAISING £80,349 IN ONE WEEK TO PROVIDE THE COST OF MOTOR TORPEDO BOAT, No. 71.

THE CITIZENS OF THE URBAN DISTRICT OF ALDRIDGE raised £80,349 in a week to provide a motor torpedo boat.

A STREET PARTY FOR VJ DAY was held on open ground opposite Broad Meadow where Walmer Meadow is now.

SECTION TEN

In the Street

ANCHOR BUILDINGS, Walsall Wood Road, showing the butchers shop.

THE ELMS HOTEL. The Anchor public house is visible at the corner of Walsall Wood Road. This photograph was taken in the 1950s.

WALSALL WOOD ROAD showing the villas and the Wesleyan Chapel. This road has been called, at other times, Lichfield Road and Anchor Lane. Three of these villas remain today. The villas were built at the turn of the century and the one nearest to the Wesleyan Chapel was used as the first Aldridge police station.

NO. 1 LEIGHSWOOD ROAD, at one time the home of Dr Stirling.

MR MARRIOT'S HOUSE which stood where the Elms Island is today. Mr Marriot can be seen in the centre of the picture. At the corner of the wall which surrounds the house there was a pump.

WALSALL WOOD ROAD showing an old gas lamp in the foreground and Mr Swain's milk cart in the distance on the right.

SOME OF THE FIRST COUNCIL HOUSES built in Aldridge in Walsall Wood Road, later demolished to make way for council flats. These council houses were very compact. In fact one of the first residents is supposed to have replied when asked if he liked them, 'Yes, they are very convenient because when I'm sitting on the toilet I can turn the bacon over at the same time.'

ROOKERY LANE. This early postcard shows the houses that once looked out over the Croft.

THE ASSEMBLY ROOMS. The building was formerly part of a farm and was later used as a meeting place. It was purchased in 1922 by Messrs B. Joberns and E. Yardley for the Aldridge Women's Unionist Association. It was renovated by W. Clare in 1926 and became known as the AWU Assembly Rooms. It was demolished in 1969.

A VIEW FROM STATION BRIDGE looking towards the village at the start of Anchor Road in the 1940s.

THE VIEW FROM THE BRIDGE in Anchor Road looking towards Beehive Cottage. This road now leads to the new by-pass.

BEEHIVE COTTAGE, situated at the end of Portland Road near the Aldridge station. It was a shop and cafe. Aldridge shoppers would have a cup of tea there on their way back from Walsall.

BANK COTTAGES, ERDINGTON ROAD.

THE SHRUBBERY, ERDINGTON ROAD, c. 1910.

THE ROBERTS GIRLS outside the family cottage in Forge Lane, 1922. Left to right: Hilda, Eva, Cissie and Florrie. The well can be seen in the foreground.

THE PINFOLD COTTAGE. This cottage stood in Erdington Road where the St Francis of Assisi Comprehensive School now stands.

WALSALL ROAD, ALDRIDGE. The White House Inn was built here, on the left, in 1937.

NORMAN MOORE'S SHOP in Walsall Road was situated opposite Aldridge Garage.

THE OLD IRISH HARP IN CHESTER ROAD. This building is over 300 years old and it is said that both Tom King and Dick Turpin were regular visitors to the inn. Aldridge tenant farmers paid their rents every six months at either the Irish Harp or the Plough and Harrow. On rent days the pubs served ale and 'rent dinners'. Irish labourers regularly used both of these public houses when potato picking at the surrounding farms.

CHESTER ROAD, Aldridge showing the Old Irish Harp on the right.

THE PLOUGH AND HARROW, Chester Road, c. 1900. Charlie Bassford, seen here with his mother, remembered seeing the Irish labourers start their day with ham and eggs and rum and coffee.

LEIGHSWOOD ROAD as it looked 100 years ago. Leighswood Avenue now opens into this road from the left.

A WINTER VIEW taken from Portland Road looking towards the Avion.

STATION ROAD.

People

MR AND MRS HERBERT outside the Pinfold Cottage, Erdington Road.

LOCAL CHARACTER MR LOVEROCK with one of his donkeys. Children could have rides in Sutton Park and also at Aldridge Agricultural Show on his donkeys.

FRANK JAMES JP became an MP for a short time in 1892.

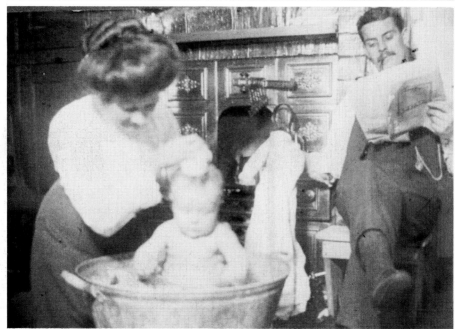

INSIDE NO. 37 BRICKYARD ROW, Leighswood Road. This unusual interior shot taken in 1913 shows Mr and Mrs Gardner and their young son at bath time. While Mrs Gardner attends to the baby, father holds the nightshirt to warm in front of the fire while reading the paper and smoking a pipe.

FLOSS AND JOE PRATT, the last occupants of the house which was once a pub known as the Rampant Lion. It was better known as the 'Romping Cat', perhaps because the painted sign outside bore more resemblance to the latter. It was situated in Erdington Road opposite the Shrubbery. It was used in the 1870s by the Irish navvies who were constructing the railway.

'COCK' DIBBLE, here holding the gun, was Aldridge's lamplighter. He is pictured in Branton Hill Lane with his son and Mr Milner.

FRANK JAMES AND MR BULL outside Portland House, which is better known today as Aldridge Court. It was called Portland House because of the use of Portland stone in its construction.

LABURNUM COTTAGES IN PADDOCK LANE. Mary Jane Davies lived there with her five sons: twins Rolf William and James Henry and Reginald, Jack and Tom.

'OLD LADY QUIMBY' outside her cottage which was next to the blacksmiths shop in Birmingham Road.

LOCAL RESIDENT CAROLINE EDWARDS, who was well known for doing good deeds and helping anyone in trouble.

MRS DAVENHILL, who still did her washing with a 'dolly tub' and old-fashioned mangle until the 1980s.

MRS TONGUE, wife of the Lord of the Manor.

THE MANOR HOUSE, built in c. 1824. This was once the home of the Tongue family. It has been used in turn as an auxiliary hospital for soldiers convalescing during the First World War, a doctor's surgery, an ambulance station and Aldridge Library but is now a youth centre.

MRS TILT, gardening at the rear of the Bassford cottages in Rookery Lane.

MR LLOYD was the Aldridge postman between 1930 and 1940.

SORTING LETTERS IN ALDRIDGE POST OFFICE. At this time the post office was situated in the High Street and was run by the Wheeler sisters.

THE ALDRIDGE COUNCIL HOUSE was built by Messrs Linford and Co. of Cannock at a cost of £4,600. The old Rural District Council had functioned for 40 years prior to the formation of the Urban District Council. When it was formed the population was 9,500 and the rateable value £42,041.

ALDRIDGE URBAN DISTRICT COUNCIL. Back row, left to right: H.B. Clay, Harold Walton, -?-, H.E. Cave, W. Emery, Mrs Harrison, -?-. Front row: Mr Nicholas, Mrs Jessie Buckley, Mr Cliff Rowley, Mr Stackhouse, Mr Partridge, -?-, Mr Buckley.

MR AND MRS GRIFFITHS OF THE SWAN. They moved to the Swan in 1939 and retired in 1964. The Swan closed in 1967.

ERNIE JORDAN OUTSIDE BAIRD'S BUTCHERS SHOP in Anchor Road, c. 1950. All the shops near the Avion were opened in the 1930s.

THE BASSFORD FAMILY photographed in Pool Green Terrace, at the rear of the cattle market.

DR JONES IN HIS SURGERY AT THE MANOR HOUSE.

CHILDREN IN FANCY DRESS, c. 1920. Doris Gardner, one of the fairies, remembers her father making the star for her wand out of a cocoa tin.

A FAMILY OUTSIDE THEIR COTTAGE IN WHARF ROW, c. 1910. These cottages were near to Wharf Bridge. The Beardsmore sisters also lived in Wharf Row and 'washed' for a living. It is said that they washed the church surplices twice a year.

ALDRIDGE FIRE SERVICE IN 1939. Mr Meek at the left on the back row was the Chief Fire Officer.

THE TIBBITS FAMILY IN THE GROUNDS OF CEDAR COURT, the family home. Fred Tibbits stands in the centre behind his wife, who is seated. Their son Cliff sits on his mother's right.

CLIFF TIBBITS was Mayor of Walsall 1939–41 and was knighted in 1948.

Rural District Council Election, 1902.

TO THE ELECTORS OF ALDRIDGE.

LADIES AND GENTLEMEN,

In again asking you for your support and vote at the coming Election, I take the liberty of bringing to your notice some of my views on questions which concern the Board of Guardians and District Council.

I will not promise the poor that their relief shall be brought to their doors, because I do not think such a thing is practical at the present time, and would add very much to the rates, but I would most certainly do all I could towards giving to the aged, and deserving poor, a larger amount of relief than is being given at present, so as to allow them to keep on their homes, and not be compelled to go to the Workhouse, as is now the case.

I should also strive to get a **Trained Nurse** appointed to live in the Parish, so that the working classes could have the benefit of her help at any time. I have long thought that this should be done in all Rural Parishes like ours.

In the appointment of a **Registrar for Births and Deaths,** I should do all that could possibly be done to appoint an Aldridge man, as I think it a great hardship for people to have to go to Walsall, as they do now, at very great inconvenience and expense to themselves.

On the District Council, I should do all I could to have those roads repaired first which needed it most, but at the same time I should not advocate spending money where it could possibly be avoided, as our rates are already too high.

I should do all I could to get the Council to use their influence with the Midland Railway Co. so as to get them to make a way from the Station into the Station Road (i.e. Red House Lane). This would be a great convenience to that District which is growing so fast.

If you should do me the honour to elect me, you may rest assured that I shall always have your interest at heart, and shall endeavour to have the spending of money, and other business connected with the District Council made more public, so that the Ratepayers may know what is being done with their money, as there seems to me far too much of this work done in Committee, of which the public know nothing whatever about.

I am, Ladies and Gentlemen,

Yours very truly,

FREDᴷ· TIBBITS.

ALDRIDGE,
March 24th. 1902.

Printed and published by W. Powis, Stafford Street Printing Works, Walsall.

FREDERICK TIBBITS' ELECTION ADDRESS.

CHARLES GEORGE BONNER (1885–1951). Son of a well-known Aldridge family, Bonner was awarded the VC 'in recognition of his conspicuous gallantry and his coolness and skill in action with enemy submarine' in October 1917. He received the award whilst spending time at Sandringham as a guest of the king and queen.

OUR VILLAGE

I remember our Village, seems so long ago
With its Shops and Cottages, all in a row.
The lovely old Church with the School beyond
And close by was a Farmhouse with ducks on the pond.

We had a little Station, I remember the smoke
When the train 'puffed in' to collect the folk.
But all these memories are now far away
They all belong to yesterday.

Today my world is a different place
Man has made progress and altered its face.
Our little Village has grown into a Town
Shops, Station, Cottages have been knocked down.

But there's a few of us left who keep a place in our hearts
For that little Country Village with its horses and carts.
We remember the Meadows, the morning dew
And those leafy woods where the bluebells grew.

Mrs A.M. Miller (eighty years an Aldridge resident)

ACKNOWLEDGEMENTS

We would like to thank all those who have loaned photographs, documents and other material and who have helped in any way with the production of this book.

BIBLIOGRAPHY

Finch Smith, J., *Notes and Collections of Aldridge*, 1889.
Fox, Betty, *Aldridge History Trail*, 1990.
Gould, James, *Men of Aldridge*, 1957.
Woodall, Richard, *Aldridge, Rushall & Pelsall Yesterdays*.

AFTERWORD

As we get older we sometimes find the rush and the roar of this fast-moving daily life trying and, perhaps, a little difficult to cope with. In order to escape from it all and to provide me with a little peace of mind, I derive great comfort recollecting the past and looking back to those much quieter days when time seemed to stand still.

We are often told to 'look to the future and not the past' but, to me, reminiscence is a worthwhile occupation and an important one for all of us. Not only do we learn and become wiser through our past mistakes; it also prevents our losing sight of the real values of the past which are still important in our everyday lives.

My own family, the Brookhouses, have a long-standing association with the village of Aldridge which stretches back several generations. I was born on 3 February 1917, one of eighteen children, in a small cottage to the rear of the Shrubbery in an area known to us all as the Romping Cat. What changes there have been since the days of that oil-lit cottage! It is the distances we have travelled which has given us the incentive to share with others, through our popular slide and talk shows, our memories of Aldridge as it once was.

We are delighted to be able to put these valuable recollections into more permanent form and to record for the benefit of future generations something of the character and history of 'old Aldridge'. We came to the conclusion some years ago that Aldridge was losing its heritage and decided to do something about it, so we visited and talked with those established citizens of Aldridge who remembered the village we did. They gave us family photographs, together with other memorabilia and information, and there the enterprise began.

John transferred the photographs to slides and we have been showing these to interested groups for the past ten years. The photographs in this selection are a sampling of our collection of over 400 views. We hope they help you share some of the pride and enthusiasm which has gone into collecting them and compiling this book – it has been a labour of love. For all those of you who go back as far as we do – 'Happy Memories'.

Stan Brookhouse
1991